*To all those who have helped me
on my journey of uncovering and healing.
I am eternally grateful.*

FOREWORD

The current edition is a reprint of the first edition with some minor changes. The original version of this book was birthed out of a workshop I designed for African American women, approximately seven years ago. However, as I continued to conduct these workshops we noticed that more men and women of other cultures were attending. Thus, it became apparent that they found the information relevant to their experiences, and helpful. Therefore, despite this book's original focus on the experiences of African American women, I believe women of various ethnicities will find it useful. This is because pain, suffering, and healing are cross-cultural experiences. Of course, this is not to imply that societal context does not influence individual encounters with these experiences. Despite the cross-cultural relevancy of the book, the original verbiage in regards to ethnicity is maintained. This permits the authenticity of the book's original purpose to be preserved.

INTRODUCTION

This book and its title were birthed out of a workshop I designed and continue to conduct predominately in church settings for African American women. Many have encouraged me for several years to write this book. I knew they were correct in their insight. However, it has taken my life some time to agree with their insight and afford the opportunity to undertake such a project. Also, I believed there was a specific aspect of my own personal journey of pain, suffering and healing I had to experience before I could embark upon this project and do it justice. The reader will notice that the book is written in the first person. Despite my many roles, licensed clinical psychologist, business owner and Christian, all of these roles are permeated by the influence of being an African American and a woman. Therefore, it would be artificial for me to try to separate myself from the pain and experiences covered in this book. I do not believe the Lord wants me to be an uninvolved bystander in this writing. None of us are exempt!

Although I realize there exists a diversity of spiritual and religious perspectives among African American women, this book is written from a Judeo-Christian perspective, which I adhere to. Thus, there are references to biblical scripture throughout the discourse. I do not apologize for the spiritual nature of this book. Spirituality and religion continue to be a significant part of the African American community, with African American women being considered the most religious/spiritual segment of American society. Our faith in God or Higher Power—greater than ourselves and beyond the influence of this universe—at times has been the primary means of getting us through some unimaginably challenging situations. Thus, I consider it apropos to write a book on emotional and mental wholeness for African American women, which is spiritual in nature. If your faith tradition is not Christian, I believe you will still find the information helpful.

This book is for African American women who have experienced or are still experiencing the emotional and mental pain and turmoil associated with all too common life situations that we encounter, such as sexual abuse, domestic violence, failed marriages, physical abuse, unfaithful partners, addicted family members, job stress, sexual assault, death of loved ones, discrimination, lost relationships and abandonment by our fathers, just to name a few. In the United States the following statistics represent the reality for many African-American women:

- In 2005-2006, 6.4% of African American women earned BA's in comparison to 3.2% of African American men. 7.1% of African American women earned Master's degrees in comparison to 2.9% of African-American men, and 3.6% of African American women earned Doctoral degrees in comparison to 1.9% of African American men.[1]

- Yet, "African-American women earn lower wages than African-American men and White women do, with White women earning a median $663 per week in 2007, compared to $629 for African-American men and $566 for African-American women. All three groups earn less than White men, whose 2007 weekly median earnings were $850."[2]

- African American women experience intimate partner violence at rates 35% higher than their White counterparts and 2.5 times the rate of men and other races.[3] Intimate partner homicide is the leading cause of death for African American women ages 15 to 45.[4]

- Also, approximately 40% of Black women report coercive contact of a sexual nature by age 18.[5]

- For every African American/Black woman who reports her rape, at least 15 African American/Black women do not report theirs.[6]

Although these situations are not confined to the experiences of women of African descent, the cultural uniqueness of our community, along with societal assumptions and attitudes about us, contributes to the uniqueness of our experiences. Navigating such situations is quite a different experience for a woman of African descent as opposed to her Euro, Latino or Asian counterparts because she is considered at the bottom of society in regards to position and power, regardless of her educational background or financial status. We live in a hostile society that bombards us—through media, education and its other major institutions—with images and implict/explict negative messages about our physical appearance, intellectual abilities, sexuality and relational abilities as wives, mothers, sisters, daughters and aunts. Many of us have accepted these negative messages and images into our mind unaware, which damage our self-worth and confidence. We have allowed these images and messages to define some aspect of who we are as women. In contrast, within the African American community, women in their roles as grandmothers, mothers, aunts, wives and sisters are expected "to always be strong" and overcome tremendous challenges in the home, family and workplace. Unfortunately, all too often our daughters, sisters, granddaughters, mothers, grandmothers and aunts find themselves in the dual roles of being the "walking wounded" and pillars of our community. This conflicting existence results in a denial of our personal woundedness and a loss of personal dreams, thrusting us into a robotic mode of survival that is bleak, lonely and without joy, hope, love or peace.

Thus, as the author it is my prayer that through reading this book, you will be inspired to begin the journey of breaking free from such an existence. Prayerfully, purchasing and reading this book represents your first step towards achieving emotional and mental wholeness. Of course it would be naïve and presumptuous to label one book as *a cure-all*. Yet, I do believe it can be as books are so often, a powerful catalyst for positive change in your life. Therefore, I encourage each reader: do not simply read to gain knowledge. Instead, read to gain understanding and wisdom about your private woundedness from past situations that continue to influence your present, thereby determining your future.

NOTES

1. National Center for Education Statistics (2008).
   Digest of Education Statistics 2007, from
   http://www.catalyst.org/publication/222/african-american-women

2. Bureau of Labor Statistics (January 2008).
   Employment and Earnings (January 2008), from
   http://diverseeducation.com/artman/publish/article_10797.shtml

3. Rennison, C. & Welchans, S. (May 2000).
   Intimate partner violence. (NJC Report No. 178247).
   Washington, DC: Bureau of Justice Statistics, from
   http://www.dvinstitute.org/

4. Campbell, J.C., Webster, D., Koziol-McLain, J. et al. (November 2003).
   Assessing risk factors for intimate partner homicide.
   NIJ Journal, 250(18), from
   http://www.dvinstitute.org/

5. National Black Women's Health Project, from
   http://www.vadv.org/secPublications/svfsaa.pdf

6. Hart and Rennison. (2003). *Bureau of Justice Statistics Special Report.*
   U.S. Department of Justice, from
   http://www.vadv.org/secPublications/svfsaa.pdf

CHAPTER 1

THE DAUGHTERS' INHERITANCES

I smell the liquor on his breath. It's dark. With each thrust, the pain shoots through my vagina and ripples through my body. I begin to cry. He tells me to be quiet and he will be finished soon. Momma is in their bedroom. I think: *Why does Daddy keep doing this? I don't understand!!! Am I such a bad little girl?* For this 10-year-old daughter, sister, and granddaughter the woundedness begins...

I did everything he asked of me. I was the devoted wife, the perfect mother. I supported the family for 2 years alone, without complaining when he was out of work. I think: *Why wasn't it enough? Why is he walking away, now? Why am I not good enough for him anymore?* The woundedness continues for this 40-year-old mother, wife...

I'm the best employee they have in this division. I work harder than anybody else and know my job. I can't believe they promoted that white woman as a supervisor over me. She's been here for two years and still does not know what she's doing. But why should I be surprised? We are the last to be hired *and promoted* and the first to be fired. *Why do I keep banging my head against this brick wall? I need to just stop trying and realize being black is a liability.* The woundedness grows for this 27-year-old employee, sister and aunt…

He told me he loved me and we would be together forever. Now I'm pregnant and he won't even answer my phone calls. Yeah, I'm acting like it's no big deal, but that's all a front. If my friends only knew how scared I really am. *Why was I so stupid and believed what he said? I'll never trust another man.* The woundedness increases for this 16-year-old daughter and soon-to-be mother…

I start crying. She tells me to shut up or she's going to hit me harder. I beg her to stop. She yells, "This is what happens to black bitches!!" *Why does Momma keep hitting me? I try to do everything right. Maybe if I just be a little more perfect, she will stop.* The woundedness continues for this 13-year-old daughter and sister…

These scenarios and the common thoughts associated with them are a sobering reminder of the painful experiences that many African American women experience. These thoughts develop into common themes, which come to define who we are as women: *the not-good-enough wife, the stupid girlfriend and the bad daughter.* The majority of us would never admit we have such thoughts. Such a confession would be extremely frightening for it represents an admittance of personal failure and weakness. It opens up the painful possibility that *I might not be as in control and together as I appear*, i.e. *I'm vulnerable*. Consequently, in an attempt to escape the pain associated with these thoughts/themes and their power over us, we push them to the dark recesses of our minds, where they come to reside. Unfortunately, this does not stop their influence. Because the pain is so great and we have only allowed it to be covered up instead of healed, it remains influencing our choices and decisions. We unknowingly begin to organize our lives around these thoughts/themes. They come to determine various aspects of our lives, such as whom we connect with, aspirations we allow ourselves to entertain, careers we pursue, and our very appearance. Unaware, we build a life on fear, pain and disappointment.

However, I believe this is the time for God's daughters—specifically African American daughters, the least among us according to societal beliefs—to receive the Father's inheritance. This belief originates from the prophetic proclamation of Numbers 27:1-7:

> *The daughters of Zelophehad son of Hepher, the son of Gilead, the son of Makir, the son of Manasseh, belonged to the clans of Manasseh son of Joseph. The names of the daughters were*

Mahlah, Noah, Hoglah, Milcah and Tirzah. They approached the entrance to the Tent of Meeting and stood before Moses, Eleazar the priest, the leaders and the whole assembly, and said, "Our father died in the desert. He was not among Korah's followers, who banded together against the LORD, but he died for his own sin and left no sons. Why should our father's name disappear from his clan because he had no son? Give us property among our father's relatives." So Moses brought their case before the LORD and the LORD said to him, "What Zelophehad's daughters are saying is right. You must certainly give them property as an inheritance among their father's relatives and turn their father's inheritance over to them."

In this scripture we have the daughters of Zelophehad asking Moses and the leaders of Israel for their father's inheritance. Their request was unorthodox and bold. Due to the gender and societal norms regarding women, they were considered less than *second-class citizens*. Therefore, they were not considered deserving of their father's inheritance. Yet, God was in agreement with Zelophehad's daughters when

Moses sought the Lord regarding their request. In the Lord's sight they were considered worthy to receive their father's inheritance. God's decision defied the societal practices of that day and challenged deeply embedded stereotypes regarding women. I believe through this scripture God is speaking prophetically to the current mental and emotional conditions of African American women. In His possession is emotional and mental wholeness, and it is our rightful inheritance. The release of an inheritance requires the death of someone. Jesus Christ's death on the cross satisfies this requirement. The atoning work Jesus accomplished on the cross was not just for salvation and physical healing but mental/emotional healing as well. Isaiah 53:4 (NIV) states:

> *Surely he took up our infirmities and carried our sorrows, yet we considered him stricken by God, smitten by him, and afflicted.*

Isaiah 53:4, King James Version states:

> *Surely he hath borne our griefs, and carried our sorrows: yet we did esteem him stricken, smitten of God, and afflicted.*

The Hebrew word for grief is *holiy khol-ee*. Its literal meaning is "malady, anxiety, calamity:--disease, grief, (is) sick(-ness)." Also, Isaiah 61:1 states:

> The Spirit of the Sovereign LORD is on me, because the LORD has anointed me to preach good news to the poor. He has sent me to bind up the brokenhearted, to proclaim freedom for the captives and release from darkness for the prisoners...

These scriptures are referring to the work of Jesus Christ as our Lord and Savior. They clearly indicate that the benefit of salvation is deliverance/healing from emotional/mental distress. Therefore, we are eligible to receive this inheritance. Neither our skin color or gender, nor the discrimination and rules of society or church disqualify us.

Like the daughters of Zelophehad, the quest by African American women for mental wholeness represents an unusual and bold request, for mental illness and participation in mental health services carries much stigma in the African American community. This is such an irony given that we as group typically encounter great stress in our lives due to the discrimination in society as well as the expectations of our community that we are the ones who should "hold things together." Yet, so many of us have sought physical healing from the Lord, and He is now saying, "Mental health is possible and available. You do not have to live a life of depression, hopelessness, guilt and shame. Healing for your woundedness is the daughter's inheritance." The time has come for us to receive our inheritance.

CHAPTER 2

WOUNDING EXPERIENCES

The mental trauma that African American women experience is real and frequent. Each of the scenarios from the previous chapter represents a brief glimpse into the negative emotional and mental impact that these experiences have on (1) how we think about ourselves and (2) our ability to develop relationships with others. There are many more, which are termed *wounding experiences*, which are situations and circumstances of life that you have encountered involving people, which result in the development of negative assumptions about yourself, other people or the world in general.

DESCRIPTION OF WOUNDING EXPERIENCES

Wounding experiences are the result of:
- The negative actions and attitudes people displayed towards you:
  - What they did or did not do
  - Expectations that they did not meet
  - Disparaging words spoken about you and/or against you

Wounding experiences can occur in a variety of settings:

- Home
- Community
- Church
- School
- Workplace or Business

The persons involved can be:

- Family members
- Friends
- Co-workers
- Church members
- Neighbors
- Strangers
- Those in authority or leadership over you – Supervisors, Pastors, Teachers, Youth Leaders

Some examples of wounding experiences include:

Abandonment	Betrayal
Spousal Infidelity	Down Low
Physical Abuse	Abortion
Adoption	Combat
Out-of-Wedlock Births	Murder
Sexual Abuse	Underemployment
Prostitution	Substance Abuse

Incest	Racism
Death of Child	Rape
Sexism	Colorism
Parental Rejection	Family Rejection
Unemployment	Church Abuse
Poverty	Pornography
Spouse/Partner Rejection	Domestic Violence
Imprisonment	Job Termination
Pastoral Abuse	Sibling Rivalry
Physical Unattractiveness	Emotional Abuse
Academic Failure	Divorce
Verbal Abuse	Discrimination

Quantity and Frequency of Wounding Events

As we consider the various causes, possible settings and people who can lead to wounding experiences, it becomes very evident that there are numerous opportunities to encounter such situations. Furthermore, the separate listing of each wounding experience gives the false impression that they occur in isolation. However, many of us have experienced several of these wounding experiences within our lifetime. Often, they have occurred at the same time. For example, we have endured emotional abuse and divorce, or discrimination and betrayal. Also, the frequency of our wounding experiences is typically more than once. The greater the number and frequency of wounding experiences, the more damaging their effect. To illustrate this point, let's take an example from my own life, which occurred when I was six years old and entering the first grade. During this time, in the area of Virginia where I lived the schools were being integrated for the first time. It was a turbulent time in the city, which I lived through. My parents, along with other African American parents, believed integrated schools were the key to a better education for their children. However, many in the Caucasian community opposed the idea. Thus, like so many other cities in America during that time, the stage was set for conflict. On the first day of school, the other kids and I arrived on our school bus, expecting to begin our first day in our new school. We were unable to exit the bus due to the presence of picketing parents and the rage they were expressing through racial epithets, name calling and other actions. The bus driver was afraid to let us off, concerned that we would be injured. Thus, we returned home. On the second day of school, we arrived once again. This time the bus entered the gated area of the school, with the school principal pad locking the gates once the bus was inside. This prevented the picketers physical access to us, allowing us to exit the bus. However, we could still hear their statements and see their rage. As a young, six-year-old child, I still recall thinking: *Why do these people hate us so much? What did we do to make them so angry, and why don't they want us at their school?* I also remember being very frightened. Throughout that school year, there were many other experiences of racism that I was subjected to. These experiences left a lasting impression on me that took many years to overcome and be healed from.

Traumatic Events

Another important factor to consider when discussing wounding experiences is that many can be considered traumatic events. These wounding experiences are extreme, severe, threatening, unpredictable, uncontrollable, all overwhelming a person's sense of safety and security and coping abilities. Traumatic events involve:

- Witnessing, or actual personal experience of, situations that consist of:
  - horror
  - helplessness
  - threat of serious injury or death
  - threat to one's physical integrity or stability
  - actual serious injury or death

- Learning about:
    o unexpected or violent death experienced by a family member or other close associate
    o serious harm experienced by a family member or other close associate
    o threat of death or injury experienced by a family member or other close associate

Some examples of traumatic events are: domestic violence, rape, sexual abuse, physical abuse, abortion, divorce, terminal illness, perceived abandonment from parents, school shootings and discrimination. Traumatic events demand an extraordinary ability to handle, which we typically do not possess. One occurrence of such an event can have a tremendous negative impact upon the mental functioning of an individual because of the inability to deal with the event, the greatest impact being that people develop various mental health disorders such as posttraumatic stress disorder or major depressive disorder.

EXERCISE 1

I encourage you to take a moment and identify the various wounding experiences you have encountered. From the list below, highlight or circle which wounding experiences you have encountered. Also, several lines are provided to write in any wounding experience that you encountered that may not be included in the list below:

Abandonment	Betrayal
Racism	Adoption
Spousal Infidelity	Prostitution
Down Low	Rape
Abortion	Combat
Out-of-Wedlock Births	Murder
Underemployment	Colorism
Sexual Abuse	Incest
Substance Abuse	Sexism
Death of Child	Divorce
Poverty	Bullying
Church Abuse	Physical Abuse
Verbal Abuse	Parental Rejection
Family Rejection	Pastoral Abuse
Physical Unattractiveness	Domestic Violence

Unemployment   Job Termination

Imprisonment   Pornography

Sibling Rivalry   Emotional Abuse

Academic Failure   Discrimination

Spouse/Partner Rejection

_____

_____

_____

_____

_____

_____

_____

_____

_____

_____

_____

_____

CHAPTER 3

WOUNDEDNESS

Regardless of type or frequency of the wounding experience, the end result is always the same emotional and mental pain. Sometimes the pain is so great and relief so unattainable, our only means of coping is to deny its existence, hoping that if we do this long enough it will disappear. Yet, it remains, always waiting for an opportunity to remind us that *I'm still here*. This pain is what I refer to as our woundedness. It is defined as the negative emotional and mental consequences of situations that you have experienced, which compromise your wholeness and well-being. It's the grave clothes that encircle you, that imprison and bind you. John 11:38-44 reads:

> *Jesus, once more deeply moved, came to the tomb. It was a cave with a stone laid across the entrance. "Take away the stone," he said. "But, Lord," said Martha, the sister of the dead man, "by this time there is a bad odor, for he has been there four days." Then Jesus said, "Did I not tell you that if you believed, you would see the glory of God?" So they took away the stone.*

Then Jesus looked up and said, "Father, I thank you that you have heard me. I knew that you always hear me, but I said this for the benefit of the people standing here, that they may believe that you sent me." When he had said this, Jesus called in a loud voice, "Lazarus, come out!" The dead man came out, his hands and feet wrapped with strips of linen, and a cloth around his face. Jesus said to them, "Take off the grave clothes and let him go."

In this passage of scripture, we have Jesus calling forth Lazarus out of the tomb. Lazarus and his circumstances represent many of us before salvation. We were dead and trapped in what appeared to be lifeless and impossible circumstances. Despite the hopelessness of our situations, God called us from the tomb, resurrecting us from spiritual death through salvation in the Lord Jesus Christ. However, when Lazarus came forth he was still wrapped in his grave clothes. He was not completely free to move about and enjoy his resurrected life. Like Lazarus many of us are still restricted by our grave clothes, our woundedness. We are saved but still emotionally and mentally bound. We are no longer in the tomb, but the remnants of the tomb—in particular our grave clothes—remain with us. It negatively impacts our behavior and spirituality, preventing us from thriving in our new resurrected life. Instead, we live an existence of maintenance and survival.

TYPES OF WOUNDEDNESS

So what is this woundedness? Although not an exhaustive list, some of the negative emotional and mental consequences of the various wounding experiences we encounter are:

Shame	Unworthiness
Insecurity	Emptiness
Confusion	Numbness
Guilt	Hopelessness
Distrust of God	Anger
Embarrassment	Self-Hatred
Powerlessness	Worry
Disappointment	Fear of Love
Recklessness	Self-Doubt
Rejection	Rage
Jealousy	Fear
Pessimism	Helplessness
Distrust of Others	Depression

Bitterness	Distrust of Self
Dislike of People	Unforgiveness
Lost	Nervousness

SEVERITY OF WOUNDEDNESS

As we examine further this passage of scripture (John 11:39, 43-44), we realize that Lazarus' restriction of movement was also determined by the tightness of his grave clothes. This tightness of grave clothes symbolizes the severity of our woundedness, the magnitude of our mental and emotional pain. The more severe our woundedness, the greater negative impact it has on our actions and spirituality. The severity of woundedness will be different for each individual depending on several factors:

- **The type of wounding experience** (i.e. what actually happened to you?) - The severity of woundedness as a result of type of wounding experience depends on: the nature of the event, what it represented for you, its meaning and how overwhelming you perceived it to be.

- **The person responsible for the wounding** (i.e. was it a stranger or a trusted love one?) - Typically, harm done by someone close will be emotionally and mentally more distressing.

- **The number of wounding experiences** (i.e. how many have you encountered?) - The greater the quantity of wounding experiences, the greater the amount of woundedness.

- **How long the experience lasted** (i.e. days, months or years?) - Ongoing wounding experiences—those that last for months or years—typically produce a greater level of woundedness.

- **Your age at the time of the experience** (i.e. were you a child, teenager or adult?) - How we think varies according to our age. Your perception of the event, how you interpret the event, who you believe was to blame for the event and why did it happen will vary depending on your age at the time of the wounding experience. These differences in our thinking ability are called cognitive development.

Cognitive Development

The most widely accepted mode of cognitive development is Piaget's, which consists of four phases. Each of these phases represents differences in our ability to understand and take in new information, depending on our age.

COGNITIVE STAGE	AGE
Sensorimotor	Birth – 2 yrs.
Preoperational	2 yrs. – 6 yrs.
Concrete Operational	7 yrs. – 11/12 yrs.
Formal Operational	11/12 yrs. - Adult

Piaget's Model

The first phase is **Sensorimotor** (birth to age 2). During this stage, as infants we learn about ourselves and the world based on our five senses and motor skills. Our five senses are touch, taste, smell, sight and sound. Thus, our thinking ability comes from the five senses and movement. For example, if we were physically abused during this time, which caused significant physical pain and injury, those sensations of pain lead us to see the world as a painful and dangerous place. This can lead to a sense of insecurity and fear.

The second phase is **Preoperational** (ages 2 to 6). During this phase, as children we learn how to use language (symbols) to explore and explain our environment. During this phase, appearance is reality. We are unable to tell the difference between fantasy and reality, which is the reason that children believe cartoons are true. Also, we are egocentric. This means that we believe the world "revolves around us" and we are personally responsible for making whatever occurs in the world happen. We are not able to perform reverse thinking at this phase. For example, we cannot comprehend that $3 + 5 = 8$ and $8-5 = 3$. Additionally, during this phase we assume that others see situations the same as we do. Therefore, we will take in information and then change it in our mind to fit our ideas. Furthermore, we have difficulty conceptualizing time. Using the example of physical abuse to see the impact of age on our thinking, such an experience during this stage often leads to self-blame because of the belief that we are responsible for what happens in our world. Thus, the woundedness of shame and unworthiness may result. If the abuser is a family member or parent, our irreversibility makes the situation extremely distressing and confusing. This distress is due to the fact that society and our personal expectations lead us to believe that parents should be good, safe people. Thus, our inability to reverse our thinking prevents us from changing our thinking of our parent from a good person to a bad person. Thus, we struggle with understanding "How could our parent, a good person, do such bad things?"

The third phase is **Concrete Operational** (ages 7 to 11 or 12). During this stage, as children we learn that appearance is *not* always reality. Also, we realize that others may have a different viewpoint and we can reverse think. However, our thinking ability is still linked to that which is real and tangible. In this phase, we do not possess the ability to think abstractly. Abstract thinking refers to the ability to consider what-ifs or think about the possibility of different ideas, solutions and outcomes about situations than what actually occurred. However, as we move towards adolescence, this ability begins to develop. Again using the physical abuse example, if we were abused during this phase we are less likely to blame ourselves because we no longer see ourselves as the center of the world and making things happen. Yet, our inability to come up with different possibilities about the situation or about how things could have been different is missing.

The fourth stage is **Formal Operational** (ages 11 or 12 to adulthood). During this stage, as adolescences/adults we are able to think abstractly and consider many possibilities from several perspectives. Also, we can mentally form theories about situations.

EXERCISE 2

I encourage you to take a moment and prayerfully determine from your previous list of wounding experiences the ten most disturbing experiences you have encountered. I have included a chart to help you with this exercise.

RANK	WOUNDING EXPERIENCE

CHAPTER 4

EFFECT OF UNRESOLVED WOUNDEDNESS

As we further examine John 11:38-44, we notice that Jesus directed the people who were present to remove Lazarus' grave clothes. The clothes did not suddenly fall away as Lazarus exited the tomb. The remnants of his death and grave experience had to be physically removed. Thus, Lazarus' resurrection experience freed him from death and the grave and positioned him to experience this removal. As African American women, God has called us from the sepulchers of our lives that wounding experiences have driven us into. Many of us are living in emotional and mental tombs, constrained by our grave clothes. Just as Mary had to endure Jesus delaying the resurrection of Lazarus, for many of us the idea of being free from our mental and emotional aguish has appeared painfully delayed. However, I believe that prophetically, God is positioning us to experience the removal of our grave clothes, the healing of our emotional and mental pain. But the question remains: Will we permit our grave clothes to be removed? Will we allow those whom Jesus directs to unwrap the woundedness that has engulfed us?

Our answer to these questions can be yes only if we desire to be healed from our woundedness. However, this means that we must be willing to confront our woundedness. Understandably, for many of us, this is a terrifying thought and usually leads to such responses as: *You must be kidding. You want me to go back and dig all that stuff up from the past? What's in the past is in the past. Some things are best left alone. I'm fine, it's over with.* Yet, despite our best efforts to convince ourselves that we do not need to address our woundedness, deep within our souls there is a part of us that recognizes that it truly is not in the past but very present and real, every day of our lives. This is so because unresolved/unhealed woundedness will always demand your attention. At the most inopportune time, when you least expect it, when you least want it to manifest, it shows up, demanding your attention in several ways, including its influence on the development of your core beliefs and your personality—the occurrence of two phenomena that I refer to as "the Wall" and "the Closet"—as well as by trauma reenactment. During the next several chapters, we will explore each of these concepts more closely.

CHAPTER 5

CORE BELIEFS
& MENTAL SCRIPTS

CORE BELIEFS (PERSONAL OPINIONS)

Core beliefs represent personal opinions about ourselves, other people and the world. These beliefs shape our emotions and actions. Woundedness flows out of the maladaptive core beliefs we develop from our various wounding experiences. The term *maladaptive* means "not productive." For example, maybe you were physically abused as a child. This wounding experience has resulted in you developing the following core beliefs: *People will always hurt you; No one will ever love me;* and *I will never be good enough.* The subsequent woundedness may be distrust of others, depression, or self-hatred. Unfortunately, as time passes our unresolved woundedness and core beliefs begin to feed off each other becoming a vicious cycle.

Wounding Experience
physically abused as a child

↓

Core Beliefs
People will always hurt you.
No one will ever love me.
I will never be good enough.

↓

Woundedness
distrust of others
fear
depression
self-hatred

Seven Common Core Beliefs of African American Women

Among African American women, researchers have identified seven common core beliefs about ourselves that are the result of the hostile environment and, thus, wounding experiences we face daily. These seven beliefs are:[1]

1) There will never be enough of anything I need, especially love.

2) I'm not good enough to be loved.

3) I'll lose anyone who gets close to me.

4) It's not safe for me to face my anger.

5) No matter what I do, it won't make a difference.

6) I have to control everyone and everything around me to protect myself from being hurt again.

7) My body is not my own.

MENTAL SCRIPTS (EXPECTATIONS ABOUT LIFE)

Core beliefs about the world, others and ourselves develop from infancy to adulthood. These beliefs and our woundedness develop into mental scripts, or what I refer to as expectations about life. Mental scripts are very similar to movie scripts that actors are required to memorize. Just like a movie script directs an actor's words, emotions, thoughts and actions, our mental scripts serve the same role in our lives. We unconsciously use them to make judgments about others, our environment and ourselves. When we do not address our woundedness and it remains unresolved, we develop negative mental scripts or expectations about life. It's through these negative mental scripts that our unresolved woundedness demands our attention. Unfortunately, they become self-fulfilling prophecies. Let's reexamine the previous example of being physically abused as a child to illustrate how mental scripts operate. This wounding experience has resulted in you developing the following core beliefs: *People will always hurt you; No one will ever love me;* and *I will never be good enough.* The subsequent woundedness may be distrust of others, depression, and self-hatred and fear. Now let's imagine you were recently hired for a new job that you desired. Typically, this situation is a time of great excitement, joy and a little nervousness. However, when you have unresolved woundedness and negative mental scripts, this is not always the case. Your expectations (mental scripts) of your new boss and co-workers might be: *My boss probably will not like me; I need to beware of my new co-workers; I just need to do my job and keep to myself; I can't do this job, what was I thinking?*

Wounding Experience
physically abused as a child

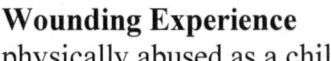

Core Beliefs
People will always hurt you.
No one will ever love me.
I will never be good enough.

Woundedness
distrust of others
fear
depression
self-hatred

Mental Scripts
My boss probably will not like me.
I need to beware of my new co-workers.
I just need to do my job and keep to myself.
I can't do this job, what was I thinking?

41

NOTES

1. Jackson, L.C., & Greene, B. (Eds.). (2000).
    Psychotherapy with African-American women: Innovations in psychodynamic perspectives and practice. New York: The Guilford Press.

CHAPTER 6

PERSONALITY GROWTH

Our personalities represent all the emotional and mental characteristics that make us who we are. When we are asked to describe people, we usually provide them with a description of someone's personality. For example, we may make such statements as: *They have a good sense of humor, They're honest, They're easygoing, They're argumentative*, or *They're negative*. However, our personality just does not appear. Just like our bodies must go through different stages of growth—infancy, toddlerhood, preschool, etc.—our personality also grows in stages. Also, similar to our bodies, the development of our personality is influenced by our environment and the life situations we encounter. For example, physically if an infant is not fed nutritious food, this can hinder his or her physical development. This is where we get the term *developmentally delayed*. Likewise, the emotional and mental impact of the environments and life situations we encounter can either hinder or enhance our personality growth. Therefore, our wounding experiences have an impact on our personality growth at the time it occurs. Also, when we allow our woundedness to remain unresolved, it continues to impact the development of our personality well beyond the age it occurred.

Erickson's Model

There are many models of personality growth. However, I prefer Eric Erikson's model of personality because it recognizes the influence of our environment, life situations and others' actions on our personality development. It also includes the idea of faith, identifies specific virtues (positive internal qualities) that are necessary for a healthy personality, and covers personality development throughout our lifetime. Due to all of these factors, Erikson's model makes it easy to understand how wounding experiences and woundedness affect our personality—the patterns of thoughts, feelings, and behaviors that make us who we are.

AGE	PERSONALITY MILESTONE	VIRTUE
Birth – 1 yr.	Basic Trust vs. Mistrust	Hope
2 – 3	Autonomy vs. Shame & Doubt	Will
4 – 5	Initiative vs. Guilt	Purpose
6 – 12	Industry vs. Inferiority	Competence
13 – 19	Identity vs. Role Confusion	Fidelity
20 – 24	Intimacy vs. Isolation	Love
25 – 64	Generativity vs. Stagnation	Care
65 – Death	Ego Integrity vs. Despair	Wisdom

Erikson's Model

This table contains Erikson's model of personality development. The model has 8 stages or phases of personality development based on age. Each of these stages involves a person facing a personality milestone. These personality milestones are defined as times of crisis in which a person is faced with the task of developing a positive trait while not completely eliminating the negative trait (e.g. Basic Trust versus Mistrust). Erikson makes it clear that there is a balance we must acquire for each stage; for example in the first stage, learning Trust is necessary. Yet, as individuals we need a healthy amount of Mistrust in order not to be naïve and vulnerable to being mistreated. If we achieve this balance, it leads to the development of a specific virtue for that stage. This in turn leads to an individual obtaining a healthy personality and the ability to successfully interact with others. If this balance is *not* achieved, the specific virtue is not achieved. Failure to successfully complete a stage results in a more unhealthy personality and the reduced ability to complete further stages. Failed stages can be resolved successfully at a later time. However, as before, this requires the individual successfully resolving the personality milestone in a positive manner.

Whether we successfully complete these stages is based on the quality of our daily social interactions with others. If those interactions were healthy and positive, we are likely to develop a balance between the positive and negative traits of that stage. This leads to us acquiring the specific virtue of that stage. Yet, if those interactions were negative and full of wounding experiences, the outcome will be an unbalanced learning of the traits. Also, the specific virtue of that stage will not be achieved. In the early stages of the model, these social interactions mainly involve our primary caregivers: parents, grandparents, aunts, uncles, foster parents or a combination of such persons. In the later stages of the model, these social interactions expand to include persons outside of our family, such as classmates, teachers or co-workers.

After the description of each stage, I have included some questions. These questions are designed to help you determine how well you completed the various stages and the impact of your woundedness on the growth of your personality. I encourage you to take the time to prayerfully and honestly answer these questions. I believe that this will begin the process of understanding how you become the person you are today.

Description of Stages

STAGE ONE – Birth to 1 Year Old

AGE	PERSONALITY MILESTONE	VIRTUE
Birth – 1 yr.	Basic Trust vs. Mistrust	Hope

The first stage of Erikson's model covers the ages from birth to one year old. The personality milestone is Trust versus Mistrust. The virtue that results if the personality milestone of Basic Trust versus Mistrust is worked out successfully is

Hope, defined as *the strong belief that, even when things are not going well, they will work out well in the end.* This Hope can be later destroyed if new pressures or conflicts arise, or strengthened by subsequent positive experiences. In this stage an infant's development of Basic Trust or Mistrust is based on the quality of care provided by his or her mother or primary caregiver. Primary caregiver refers to the person who was responsible for raising you as a child. This may have been an aunt, grandmother or father. The quality of care must consist of familiarity, consistency, and continuity. An example of quality care on the part of the caregiver would be that when the infant cries, he or she readily, regularly and effectively response to the infant's need. This teaches the infant that the world is a responsive and predictable place and others are dependable. The infant gains confidence and security through the interactions with his or her caregiver. Therefore, the primary caregiver acting in a loving and consistent manner and meeting the infant's needs leads to the development of Basic Trust.

Erikson felt this Basic Trust becomes the capacity for Faith. However, if parents are overly protective, responding immediately to the infant's first cry. This results in the infant being overly trusting or gullible and never achieving a balance of Basic Trust versus Mistrust. In contrast, if the primary caregiver acts in an unreliable, distant, unresponsive and rejecting manner towards the infant, this results in the infant becoming frustrated and angry. The infant learns that others are unreliable and uncaring. This feeling of being deprived will lead to Mistrust being the major attitude the infant develops. Therefore, too much trust or too much mistrust results in the virtue of Hope not being achieved. The achievement of a proper balance between Trust versus Mistrust, leads to the development of Hope. This Hope is what later in life helps us to overcome the many disappointments of life.

QUESTIONS FOR THOUGHT: As you think about your early years of life, what kind of primary caregivers did you have? Were they loving, kind and reliable? Or harsh, absent and inconsistent?

STAGE TWO – 2 to 3 Years Old

AGE	PERSONALITY MILESTONE	VIRTUE
2 – 3	Autonomy vs. Shame & Doubt	Will

The second stage of Erikson's Model covers the ages from two to three years old. The personality milestone is Autonomy versus Shame and Doubt. If this stage is worked out successfully the child will achieve a degree of Autonomy while minimizing Shame and Doubt. The virtue that results if the personality milestone of Autonomy versus Shame and Doubt is resolved successfully is Will, defined as *the unbroken determination to exercise free choice as well as self-restraints.* In this stage children begin to exercise their independence and will. The challenge of this stage for primary caregivers is teaching children to obey while allowing them to be assertive and exercising their independence. For example such tasks as allowing children to choose what to eat or what toy to play with are common ways of allowing children to be independent.

A sense of Autonomy or self-control will emerge if parents guide their children's behavior gradually & firmly, encouraging their independence. Also, a sense of self-esteem (feeling good about yourself) will emerge. This leads to Will. The child becomes confident in the ability to survive in the world. However, children will experience a sense of defeat, if the primary caregiver is too permissive, harsh and/or demanding and overly helpful during this stage. This leads to Shame and Doubt concerning their ability to make effective judgments and exercise control over their lives and their self-worth. Again, a balance of Autonomy versus Shame and Doubt is needed. The lack of Shame and Doubt leads to **impulsiveness**. Erikson defined impulsiveness as a sort of shameless willfulness that leads you in later childhood and even adulthood to jump into things without proper consideration of your abilities. In contrast, too much shame and doubt leads to **compulsiveness**. This is a sense that who you are is defined by what you do. Thus, everything must be done perfectly and mistakes avoided at all cost.

QUESTIONS FOR THOUGHT: As you think about your early childhood, what kind of primary caregivers did you have? Were they overly protective, harsh, lacking patience, not tolerant of any mistakes? Or did they create an environment that allowed you to try new things, make choices and explore?

STAGE THREE – 4 to 5 Years Old

AGE	PERSONALITY MILESTONE	VIRTUE
4 – 5	Initiative vs. Guilt	Purpose

The third stage of Erikson's Model covers the ages from four to five years old. The personality milestone is Initiative versus Guilt. The goal of this stage is to achieve an adequate amount of Initiative with minimal Guilt. Initiative is defined as a positive response to life's challenges, taking on responsibilities and learning new skills. The virtue that results if the personality milestone of Initiative versus Guilt is resolved successfully is Purpose, defined as *thinking big, identifying with parents and setting major life goals.* This stage is about children beginning to explore what type of person or adult they will grow up to be. Children begin to play make-believe games such as house and dress up, imitating adult roles in their quest to determine what kind of adult they will be. They also ask endless "how and why" questions about the world.

If parents respond in an understanding manner and guide the child's motives and desires into socially acceptable activities, the child will develop a healthy sense of Initiative with minimal Guilt. However, if parents ridicule, shame or belittle the child for their play acting or pretending and discourage their dreaming, the child will develop a sense of Guilt for attempting to dream and desiring to explore and satisfy their curiosity about being an adult. Also, if the parent rushes or demands the child to grow up or become an adult too soon, this can lead to an excessive amount of Initiative. Once again, balance is the goal of this stage. Too much Guilt will lead to what Erikson referred to as **inhibition**. Erikson described this as a fear of exploration and attempting to become or accomplish things. Erikson believed excessive initiative leads to **ruthlessness**. He described this as the tendency by people to carry out their plans (career, academic, social) without regard for others. In essence, such people do not care whom they hurt in the process of achieving their goals.

QUESTIONS FOR THOUGHT: As you think about your childhood at this age, what were your primary caregivers like? Did they ridicule or make you feel ashamed for asking questions, dreaming about what type of job you wanted to have as an adult? Or did they encourage you to go after your dreams and to believe in yourself?

STAGE FOUR– 6 to 12 Years Old

AGE	PERSONALITY MILESTONE	VIRTUE
6 – 12	Industry vs. Inferiority	Competence

The fourth stage of Erikson's Model covers the ages from six to 12 years old. The personality milestone is Industry versus Inferiority. The goal of this stage is to achieve Industry while avoiding excessive Inferiority. The virtue that results if the personality milestone of Industry versus Inferiority is managed successfully is Competence, defined as *feeling that one is adequate, capable of achieving and learning.* This virtue prepares youth for future roles in job settings. The sense of Industry has to do with learning how to complete jobs. During this time, youths are busy learning academic, athletic and social skills, which enable them to be good students, athletes and peers. These are the jobs they are trying to complete. At this stage teachers become the center of a child's life. This occurs because teachers are introducing them to new knowledge and technology about the world, which prepares them for their future.

It is important that youths in this stage experience success and what that feels like. If parents and teachers demonstrate encouragement and care and peers are accepting of the youth, they are likely to have such success and subsequently develop an adequate sense of Industry with minimal Inferiority. In contrast, several factors will lead to a sense of Inferiority. These factors include: the child fails to learn new things or the child is prevented from learning new things due to the chaos of his or her environment or harsh teachers, rejection by peers, racism, sexism and other forms of discrimination. Erikson felt discrimination leads to Inferiority because it teaches a child that success is based on who you are rather than your ability and how hard you work. Since I cannot change my skin color or gender, then why try to be successful? In contrast, too much Industry results in what Erikson called **narrow virtuosity,** which is described as the tendency by parents to pressure their children into focusing on one area of achievement while ignoring other interests. Examples of this include child actors, athletes and prodigies.

QUESTIONS FOR THOUGHT: As you think about your childhood at this age, who were the most influential people in your life? Was it a teacher, coach or relative? How did these people treat you? Were they kind and encouraging of your abilities/talents? Did they discourage your talents? Were you liked by other children? Did you encounter prejudice or discrimination which stopped you from developing abilities or pursuing interests?

STAGE FIVE– 13 to 19 Years Old

AGE	PERSONALITY MILESTONE	VIRTUE
13 – 19	Identity vs. Role Confusion	Fidelity

The fifth stage of Erikson's Model covers the ages from 13 to 19 years old. The personality milestone is Identity versus Role Confusion. The goal of this stage is to achieve an Identity while avoiding Role Confusion. Identity involves *the things we are, the things we want to become and the things we are supposed to become, along with the things we do not want to be and the things, which we know we are not supposed to be.* In essence, Identity refers to knowing who you are and your place in society. Role Confusion refers to *an identity* crisis *about who we are and what we will become, an uncertainty about one's place in society and the world.* The virtue that results if the personality milestone of Identity versus Role Confusion is resolved successfully is Fidelity, which is defined as *the ability to freely connect and be loyal to people despite differences in value systems, the ability to commit and be loyal to a vision of the future and move to meet it.* During this stage, adolescents are becoming more independent. They are beginning to look at the future in terms of career choices, lifestyle choices, partner choices, which values and principles to follow and residence choices. If an adolescent has successfully worked out the previous stages, they enter this stage with a growing sense of who they are. Such adolescents have been fortunate to receive from their primary caregivers affirmation regarding their self-worth, knowing that they are an important part of the family. Also, such adolescents have been exposed to various cultural experiences, which provided them with a sense of direction and uniqueness. Additionally, they have a healthy sense of independence and personal effectiveness. All of these factors will aid such adolescents in the successful resolution of this stage.

In contrast, if the previous stages have not been resolved successfully, the adolescent will often enter this stage with feelings of inadequacy and incompetence due to past failures. There will also be feelings of guilt and shame because of previous actions. This youth will find it particularly difficult to develop a clear sense of Identity and avoid Role Confusion. Erikson believed that good adult role models, open lines of communication with parents/primary caregivers, and societal rites of passages practice would be helpful for adolescents to develop a healthy sense of Identity. If these things are absent from a youth's life, the likelihood of Role Confusion increases. Unfortunately, the absence of a clear sense of identity often leads to a range of negative emotional states: pessimism, boredom, unfocused anger, personal confusion, helplessness and hopelessness. Also, Role Confusion may lead to youths acting in a hostile manner towards societal roles seen as proper and desirable, such as being parents, teachers, community leaders, police officers. Consequently, their loyalties may be turned to groups and ideas that are destructive to themselves and society, such as gangs, terrorist groups, extremist, racist groups or counter-cultures such as Goths. As always, Erikson felt balance was the key. Therefore, he does believe a person can have too much Identity. This involves a situation in which we are so immersed in a specific role in society that we do not have any tolerance for others who oppose our roles or the ideas they represent. Erikson labeled this excessive amount of Identity as **fanaticism**, a fanatic being one who believes his or her way of life is the only and right way.

QUESTIONS FOR THOUGHT: As you think about your teenage years, what type of person were you? Were you confident, outgoing, kind and friendly? Or shy, insecure, angry or fearful?

STAGE SIX– 20 to 24 Years Old

AGE	PERSONALITY MILESTONE	VIRTUE
20 – 24	Intimacy vs. Isolation	Love

The sixth stage of Erikson's Model covers the ages from 20 to 24 years old. This stage is referred to as *young adulthood*. The personality milestone is Intimacy versus Isolation. The goal of this stage is to achieve some level of Intimacy while minimizing Isolation. Intimacy is defined as *the ability to establish close relationships with others, to be involved in enduring, committed relationships*. This does not necessarily mean a sexual relationship. Isolation is defined as *the inability to take chances with one's identity by sharing true intimacy*. If the personality milestone of Intimacy versus

Isolation is resolved positively, the virtue of Love is achieved. Erikson defined Love as *the ability to put aside difference and antagonisms by "mutuality of devotion."* This stage has to do with our quest for mutually satisfying relationships, mainly through marriage and friendship. The development of a healthy sense of identity is necessary for entering this stage. Therefore, a person's inability to successfully resolve Stage Five prevents him or her from entering this stage and acquiring true Intimacy. This is due to the fact that truly intimate relationships are only possible between two people who have clearly established identities and loyalties. If we achieve too much Intimacy, it leads to what Erikson calls **promiscuity**, which is the tendency to be too free and easy in becoming intimate without any depth to the intimacy. If we experience too much Isolation, **exclusion** emerges. This is the tendency to isolate yourself from love, friendship and community, as well as developing hatefulness as a means of compensating for your loneliness.

QUESTIONS FOR THOUGHT: As you think about your young adulthood years, what was the usual quality of your relationships and friendships? Did you have friendships and relationships that were supportive, loving and strong? Or were they violent, hostile or shallow? Which type of relationships and friendships did you prefer? What type of relationships and friendships do you desire now?

STAGE SEVEN– 25 to 64 Years Old

AGE	PERSONALITY MILESTONE	VIRTUE
25 – 64	Generativity vs. Stagnation	Care

The seventh stage of Erikson's Model covers the ages from 25 to 64 years old. This stage is referred to as *middle adulthood*. The personality milestone is Generativity versus Stagnation. The goal of this stage is to achieve a balance between these two traits. If this goal is achieved, the virtue Care will be acquired. Care is defined as *the widening concern for what has been generated by love, necessity or accident.* The main focus of this stage is the establishment and guidance of the next generation. Generativity involves *the production and rearing of children, as well as the creation of products, ideas, and other things that can be used to benefit others.* Stagnation represents the opposite of Generativity. It is *the lack of productivity: boredom and relational poverty.* If you become too generative, it leads to **overextension**. Erikson describes overextension as the practice of being too giving and involved with meeting the needs of others, without allowing time for yourself to rest and relax. The opposite of this is **rejectivity**, which is when we have an excessive amount of stagnation, leading us to not contributing to others or participating in society.

QUESTIONS FOR THOUGHT: As you think about your adulthood years, what has been the main focus? Is it to get all you can for yourself, or to give back to others and/or society? Do you have a hard time saying *no* to others?

STAGE EIGHT– 65 Years Old to Death

AGE	PERSONALITY MILESTONE	VIRTUE
65 – Death	Ego Integrity vs. Despair	Wisdom

The final stage of Erikson's Model covers the ages from 65 years to death. This stage is called *late adulthood*. The personality milestone is Ego Integrity versus Despair. The goal is to develop Ego Integrity with minimal Despair. If this stage is successfully resolved, you will acquire Wisdom, defined as *meaningful old age*. This stage is an intense time of reflection and recollection of memories and dreams. It also involves your attempts to make meaning of your life while coming to terms with your imminent death. Also, you will be faced with the physical changes in their bodies, the death of love ones and possible personal illnesses.

Healthy individuals at this stage are able to adapt to the triumph and disappointments of life, be productive, establish meaning and purpose, and accept the fact that death is a natural part of life. You do not fear death. This is Ego Integrity: *seeing a unity and meaning in your life and coming to terms with your life and death.* However, too much Ego Integrity results in **presumption**. This is the tendency to present the façade of Ego Integrity without really coming to terms with the difficulties of old age and being honest with yourself. Despair is *the realization that life is now short and you have wasted your life and don't have any time to start a new life or attempt new paths to integrity.* If you develop too much Despair, this will lead to **disdain,** which is contempt for life in general, yours and others.

QUESTIONS FOR THOUGHT: If you have reached this age, how much regret are you experiencing about your past? Are you able to look back over your life and be honest about your success and failure? Do you hate thinking about your life? If you have yet to reach this age, how do you feel right now about your life up to this point? Are you pleased with the choices you have made? Are you proud about the type of life you have lead so far? What do you need to do different?

CHAPTER 7

THE WALL

As we mentioned earlier, the third way unresolved woundedness demands our attention is "the Wall." When we allow our woundedness to continue unhealed, it becomes the bricks by which we mentally build an invisible wall, one that serves as a fortress to keep out all those persons whom we think may hurt us or reject us. When we emotionally and mentally create the Wall in our lives, there are several questions that are always in the back of our minds whenever we meet or interact with someone. These questions are: *Are you going to hurt me? Are you going to reject me? Are you going to do the bad things that other's have done to me?* Thus, the Wall is a way we attempt to emotionally protect ourselves. Unfortunately, though the Wall may provide us with this protection, it also causes us to be emotionally distant from others. This leaves us in a state of isolation, never being able to really share ourselves with someone—who we *really* are— never allowing us to be vulnerable. Consequently, the Wall often leaves us lonely and emotionally bankrupt because it does not allow us to receive love, support and emotional satisfaction from the various relationships in our life. In short, the Wall hinders our ability to form intimacy in relationships.

Although the Wall may protect us from being hurt or rejected by others, it also leaves us feeling emotionally empty and still wounded since we do not permit others to pour into us the support, love, understanding and kindness, which would help us to heal.

Spiritually, the Wall shuts you off from the love of God as well. Mentally, you may know that God loves you, but the Wall prevents it from becoming a heartfelt truth. The Wall prevents God's love (or as I often say, Love's love—for God *is* love) from penetrating your woundedness with the light of His love. This often happens because without realizing it, we are asking God the same questions: *Are you going to reject me? Are you going to hurt me?* In the most severe instances of unhealed woundedness, the questions become for God and others: *When are you going to hurt me? When are you going to reject me? When are you going to let bad things happen to me?* Thus, we go through life trying to barricade ourselves from, or brace ourselves for, the next wounding experience.

When we allow ourselves to build the Wall, we will often hear the people in our lives (spouses, siblings, parents, etc.) make such statements about us as: *She's so cold. She's a nice person but you can't get close to her, don't mind her she's just strange.* Or, we may experience family and friends asking us: *Will you ever let me in? What is it going to take for you to trust me?* Such statements and questions only perpetuate our feelings of rejection, loneliness and being misunderstood. It increases our woundedness. Therefore, it provides us with more bricks to make the Wall in our lives higher and thicker. This shuts us off even more from the people in our lives with whom we could have emotionally fulfilling relationships. Thus, we find ourselves in a vicious cycle of emotional emptiness. This often leads to us developing a sense of hopelessness about ever having any type of emotionally fulfilling relationship. Often, the end result is that we either completely shut ourselves off from others, or we begin to settle for whatever/whomever in our various types of relationships: marital, romantic, family or friends. We begin to ignore how bad a person treats us because we really do not believe that we can achieve or deserve any better.

QUESTIONS FOR THOUGHT: Have you built the Wall in your life? What areas of woundedness were used to build the Wall? Who's love, support and kindness is the Wall keeping you from receiving? What hurtful relationships/people are you tolerating because of the Wall?

CHAPTER 8

THE CLOSET
& TRAUMA REENACTMENT

"The Closet" is the fourth way in which unresolved/unhealed woundedness demands our attention. The Closet is the place we emotionally and mentally create to hide our woundedness. It is an invisible place within ourselves that is stuffed with all the woundedness of our past and present that we try to conceal from the outside world, denying its impact on us. It is our hiding place. However, unlike the hiding place of the Lord, it is not a place of comfort, refreshing or safety. It's a place of fear and secrecy. The Closet represents our attempt to present the façade that *I am okay. I've gotten past that. It is over.* It requires a lot of emotional and mental energy from us to keep stuff hidden and shut up in our Closet. Thus, keeping stuff in the Closet makes us tired and hinders us from enjoying our life. Also, like any real closet when it becomes too full and we open the door, things tend to fall out. The same is true about our invisible Closet. At the most inconvenient times, our woundedness tends to fall out. In the midst of us trying to establish a healthy romantic relationship, for example, mistrust falls out, stopping us in our tracks. While trying to pursue a new job, rejection tumbles out, convincing us to give up. While trying to walk away from an abusive relationship, self-hatred hits us on the head, convincing us "I deserve this" and stops us from leaving. The more woundedness we stuff in the Closet, the more dangerous a place it becomes. The danger increases because it creates more opportunity for stuff to "fall out" in the midst of our daily lives.

QUESTIONS FOR THOUGHT: What's in your Closet? How full is your Closet? What are you willing to take out of your Closet?

Trauma Reenactment

Trauma reenactment is the final way in which unresolved/unhealed woundedness demands our attention. A traumatic event is a wounding experience which is extreme, severe, threatening, unpredictable, and/or uncontrollable, overwhelming a person's sense of safety and security and coping abilities. Some examples of traumatic events are domestic violence, rape, and the sudden death of a love one. Traumatic events have a great impact on us emotionally and mentally. When we go through such experiences in our attempt to be healed from them, we try to make meaning of the event. Making meaning of such events is the way we try to regain emotional and mental balance. This is a normal reaction and usually involves us asking ourselves such questions as: *Why did this happen? Why did I survive? Why did this happen to me and not someone else? What was its purpose? Why did God let this happen? How do I move on from this? Why did I stay there?* Yet, sometimes we try to figure out the meaning of traumatic events in an unhealthy way, especially when help is not available. This brings us to the idea of trauma reenactment. Trauma reenactment is an unhealthy way of trying to make meaning out of our trauma. It involves us making decisions and behaving in ways which lead to the reoccurrence of the same emotional and mental pain as the original traumatic event. It is something we do automatically and unknowingly. In other words, we are unaware that we are repeating the emotional and mental pain of the trauma over and over in our lives. Unfortunately, trauma reenactment leads to us to performing very self-destructive actions. One example of trauma reenactment is the sexually abused young girl who becomes involved in having unprotected sex with many, many partners. In this case the young girl is repeating the feelings of being worthless, unloved, taken advantage of and self-hatred, which are so often the outcome of being sexually abused. Another example is the battered woman who continues to go from one abusive relationship to another. In this case this woman is repeating the feelings of rejection, shame, hopelessness, powerlessness, self-hatred and worthlessness, which are so often the result of being battered. A third example is the physically abused teenager who is always putting herself in dangerous/deadly situations. In this example, the teenager is repeating the feelings of fear, death, worthlessness and rage that usually result from physical abuse.

QUESTIONS FOR THOUGHT: Are you repeating the emotional and mental pain of past wounding experiences by your choices and actions? If so, what are the painful emotions or thoughts you are repeating?

CHAPTER 9

IT'S TIME TO REPLENISH THE OIL

2 Kings 4:1-7 reads as follows:

The wife of a man from the company of the prophets cried out to Elisha, "Your servant my husband is dead, and you know that he revered the LORD. But now his creditor is coming to take my two boys as his slaves." Elisha replied to her, "How can I help you? Tell me, what do you have in your house?" "Your servant has nothing there at all," she said, "except a little oil." Elisha said, "Go around and ask all your neighbors for empty jars. Don't ask for just a few. Then go inside and shut the door behind you and your sons. Pour oil into all the jars, and as each is filled, put it to one side." She left him and afterward shut the door behind her and her sons. They brought the jars to her and she kept pouring. When all the jars were full, she said to her son, "Bring me another one." But he replied, "There is not a jar left." Then the oil stopped flowing. She went and told the man of God, and he said, "Go, sell the oil and pay your debts. You and your sons can live on what is left."

In this book we have described wounding experiences and woundedness. Also, we have examined separately each of the ways unhealed woundedness demands our attention or continues to influence our lives. These ways include: the influence of woundnedness on the development of our core beliefs and our personality, the occurrence of the Wall, the Closet and trauma reenactment. Yet, in reality each of these concepts does not occur in our lives separately. They interact with each other, influencing our core beliefs, which in turn impacts our personality growth, which re-impacts our core belief, which in turn influences the Closet, which influences the Wall. In essence, unhealed woundedness sets us up for this vicious cycle of continuous impact. Prayerfully, reading this book has helped you to gain a better understanding of your woundedness and the areas of your life that need healing. Yet, so often a better understanding of our emotional and mental pain leaves us with doubts about our ability to be healed. Like the widowed woman, the cares of this world and life circumstances may have left you feeling empty, dry, hopeless and helpless. But it's time to receive your inheritance.

That inheritance is the replenishing of the oil. God does not desire for you to remain emotionally destitute and bankrupt. As with the widow in the text, He desires to give you, your inheritance of emotional and mental healing, which is the replenishing of your oil. This replenishing will be gradual but steady, as you follow the leading of the Lord in taking steps towards your healing. Elisha is a type, or representation, of Jesus Christ. He gave the widow clear instructions as to what actions she should take to solve her problem of lack, how to replenish her oil. I believe the Lord is more than willing to give you clear instructions on how to solve your lack of mental and emotional wholeness.

How to bring about your healing? Like the widow, seek out help. Do not try to travel this road alone. If the widow had not sought out help or ignored the instructions of the prophet, her sons would have been taken into slavery and she would have remained destitute, in debt. The fruit of her womb—those whom she had birthed—her dreams, vision, purpose, destiny would all have been taken captive, along with herself. This is what unhealed woundedness does: along with yourself, it takes captive your fruitfulness, your dreams, vision and purpose.

I encourage you to ask the Lord about the path you should take for your healing. For some of you, this path may involve seeking help from a mental health professional (licensed counselor, licensed psychologist, licensed clinical social worker or licensed pastoral counselor). For others it may mean a time of prayer, fasting and increased time in the Word of God. For others the path may include seeking the prayer support of others. For many it will involve all of these methods. Regardless of the path the Lord directs you down, the most important thing is that you stay on it. Do not give up and do not be ashamed. God loves you and because of His love, He desires that you be healed, not just physically but emotionally and mentally. Let His love bring about the wholeness you so desperately desire. Ephesians 3:20-21 reads:

Now to him who is able to do immeasurably more than all we ask or imagine, according to his power that is at work within us, to him be glory in the church and in Christ Jesus throughout all generations, for ever and ever! Amen.

CHAPTER 9

RESOURCES

Listed below are organizations that address various needs of African American Women. Free Internet access is available through your local public library.

**National Organization of Sisters
of Color Ending Sexual Assault**
http://www.sisterslead.org/
(860) 693-2031

**Institute on Domestic Violence
in the African American Community**
http://www.dvinstitute.org/
(877) 643-8222

National Council of Negro Women, Inc.
http://www.ncnw.org/
(202) 737-0120

Black Career Women's Network
https://bcwnetwork.com
(513) 729-9724

Listed below are organizations and their websites, which maintain directories of counselors, psychologists and social workers:[1]

Christian Association for Psychological Studies

http://www.caps.net/

(630) 639-9478

American Association of Christian Counselors

http://www.aacc.net/

(800) 526-8673

National Christian Counselors Association

http://www.ncca.org/

(941) 388-6868

American Psychological Association

http://www.apa.org/

(800) 374-2721

National Association of Social Workers

http://www.socialworkers.org/

(202) 408-8600

If you have health insurance, you can also go to its website and find a mental health provider, according to the specific criteria (gender, ethnicity, area of specialty, location) you select.

1. *Dr. Portia Rawles does not examine, determine, or provide a warranty with respect to the competence of any counselor, psychologist or social worker listed in the above directories. User agrees that User's use of the directories to locate a counselor, psychologist or social worker is wholly voluntary and the user further agrees that User's use of the directories or a counselor, or reliance on the advice or direction of a counselor, psychologist or social worker shall not result in any liability against Dr. Rawles. In no event shall Dr. Rawles be liable for damages to any user of the directories for the selection of any counselor, psychologist or social worker for the services provided by any listed counselor, psychologist or social worker or for any damages which may occur relating to the use of the directories or counselor, psychologist or social worker.*

ABOUT THE AUTHOR

Dr. Portia Rawles, a licensed clinical psychologist and licensed minister, is the developer of and facilitator for the *Uncovering and Healing Your Woundedness* workshop. Dr. Rawles received her bachelor's degree from Stanford University and her doctorate from Regent University. As a psychologist, Dr. Rawles serves in the capacity of clinician, presenter, professor, consultant and researcher. Dr. Rawles also worked in the capacity of a college professor. She formerly served for five years as an Assistant Professor of Psychology in the Doctor of Psychology (Psy.D.) program at Regent University, specializing in Multicultural Psychology, the Psychology of Trauma and Crisis, and Clinical Practica.

Due to her faith background, as a born-again Christian with numerous ministry experiences, Dr. Rawles has a special passion in integrating biblical and psychological principles to meet the needs of women and children experiencing trauma-related mental health disorders within the African American community. Her ministry experiences include missionary work in Nigeria as a part of a 14-member missionary team, Sunday school teacher, women's ministry co-founder, pulpit speaker, intercessory/altar prayer team member, youth ministry leader, and outreach ministries to the disadvantaged such as the homeless, substance abusers and AIDS victims.

Dr. Rawles is also the founder of Rawles and Associates, PLC as well as Covenant Place. Rawles & Associates, PLC is a mental health organization committed to providing quality, clinical, consulting, training and presentation services. The clinical focus of Rawles & Associates, PLC is meeting the needs of at-risk individuals experiencing trauma-related mental health disorders, especially within the African American community. Covenant Place was a faith-based therapeutic group home for adolescent girls who have been sexually and/or physically abused.

WORKSHOP

If you would like for Dr. Rawles to conduct an *Uncovering and Healing Your Woundedness* workshop or wish to learn more:

Dr. Portia Rawles

Tel: (757) 493-2912

Web: http://DrPortiaRawles.com

Email:info@DrPortiaRawles.com

Facebook: Facebook.com/DrPortia

Twitter: Twitter.com/DrPortia1